The Expertise Connection

Transforming Conversations into Client Commitment

Kenneth M. Rollins

All rights reserved. No part of this publication may be reproduced, distributed, or transmitted in any form or by any means, including photocopying, recording, or other electronic or mechanical methods, without the prior written permission of the publisher, except in the case of brief quotations embodied in critical reviews and certain other noncommercial uses permitted by copyright law. Copyright © (Kenneth M. Rollins), (2024).

Table of Contents

Introduction 1
Part 1: The Foundation of Effective Conversations 8
The Psychology of Decision-Making 9

From Selling to Guiding 17
Part 2: The Four Conversations 26
Conversation 1: Discovery.. 26
Conversation 2: Insight 36
Conversation 3: Partnership... 47
Conversation 4: Commitment 58
Part 3: Applying the Model 68
Adapting the Four Conversations to Different Contexts 68
Overcoming Objections and Challenges: Handling Resistance and Hesitation Effectively 80
The Future of Selling Expertise: Why Conversations Will Always Matter in a Digital Age 101
Summary: The Expertise Connection—Transforming Conversations into Client Commitment......................................110
Appendices: A Practical Toolkit for Mastering Conversations 116

-
-

-
-
-

-
-

Introduction

Why Expertise Requires a New Sales Model

Experts face challenges in traditional sales.

Experts often disagree with established sales approaches. Why? Because such models were not created for individuals who value knowledge, insight, and problem-solving. Traditional sales focus on volume, transactions, and persuasion. They thrive on rapid successes and elevator pitches, which contrast with experts' deliberate, nuanced approaches.

As an expert, you're probably not interested in being seen as a salesman. You're enthusiastic about solving complicated challenges, providing innovative solutions, and serving as a trusted adviser. However, this enthusiasm may occasionally work against you in a sales situation. Clients may be overwhelmed by too much information or technical intricacies. They may fail to see the link between your level of experience and their current demands.

What was the result? Frustration. You wonder, "Why can't they see the value I bring?" Meanwhile, the customer thinks, "Why can't this person simply tell me how they can help?" The divide is genuine and persistent.

Understanding the value of conversations over pitches.

This is when the power of discussion comes in. Conversations, as opposed to typical pitches, are interactive and two-way. They enable both sides to explore, discover, and co-create solutions.

A pitch is generic, but a discussion is individualized to

the individual. A pitch informs, but a discussion finds. A pitch aims to convince, but a discussion fosters trust. And trust is the foundation of sales competence.

Clients want more than just a transaction in an increasingly skeptical world of sales methods. They want partnerships. They want to be heard, understood, and valued. They are not searching for someone to sell to; rather, they are seeking someone to partner with.

The Four Conversations paradigm accepts this fact. It changes the emphasis from promoting a product or service to encouraging meaningful discourse. This strategy not only improves the customer experience but also allows specialists to sell in a manner that is consistent with their beliefs and skills.

Overview of the Four Conversations Model.

The Four Conversations model is a structure that helps professionals navigate the sales process while maintaining their authenticity and competence.

1. Discovery: This is where the trip starts. It's all about asking the appropriate questions and fully understanding the client's situation.
2. Insight - Here, you show your worth by providing fresh views and clarifying the client's issues.
3. Partnership - During this phase, you and the customer work together to find solutions, establishing a spirit of teamwork.
4. Commitment - Finally, you help the customer to a conclusion, making sure they feel secure and supported in their choice.

Each interaction is a step forward, intended to increase trust, deepen understanding, and eventually lead to a mutually beneficial partnership.

2. The Experts' Dilemma
Balancing Credibility and Relatability

Experts refuse to compromise their credibility. It is what distinguishes you and makes your counsel worth paying for. But credibility isn't enough. To market your skills, you must be relatable. Clients must have a connection with you before they will trust your advice.

This balance may be challenging. On the one hand, you want to demonstrate your breadth of expertise and experience. On the other hand, you don't want to come out as distant or too intellectual. A customer who feels frightened or detached will not participate, regardless of how bright you are.

Empathy, curiosity, and humility are the root causes of relatability. It is about meeting customers where they are, not where you believe they should be. It's about explaining complicated ideas without seeming condescending. And it is about demonstrating that you understand their challenges, not just intellectually but realistically.

Achieving this equilibrium requires self-awareness and adaptation. It entails being sensitive to the client's communication style and emotional indicators. It entails understanding when to lead with arguments and when to lead with tales.

Overcoming Client Misconceptions about Expertise.

Another issue for experts is dealing with misunderstandings about what knowledge entails and how much it is worth. Some consumers may underestimate competence since they may not completely comprehend it. Others may associate knowledge with rigidity, believing that an expert would push a pre-packaged solution rather than listening to their specific requirements.

Even before the debate starts, these assumptions might spark skepticism or resistance. Your job is to gently break down these barriers by redefining what expertise looks like in action.

Show, don't tell. Instead of listing your credentials, demonstrate your expertise by asking thoughtful questions and providing relevant insights.

Keep your options open. Emphasize your ability to apply your knowledge to the client's specific circumstances.

Address concerns directly. If a client appears hesitant, ask why. This demonstrates that you are not only an expert, but also a partner who values their opinions.

Finally, the expert's issue is an opportunity rather than an impediment. You may position yourself as a trustworthy counselor and valued partner by mastering the art of blending credibility and relatability and confronting misunderstandings front on.

This introduction sets the setting for an engaging examination of the Four Conversations concept, emphasizing why it is important and how it tackles the particular problems of selling knowledge. The idea is to fascinate the reader while delivering practical insights that they can instantly use in their situations.

Part 1: The Foundation of

Effective Conversations

The Psychology of Decision-Making

Understanding how customers make purchasing choices is both an art and a science. While skill and reasoning play important roles, they are not the only driving forces. Human decision-making is heavily impacted by emotions, social dynamics, and subconscious impulses. To successfully offer knowledge, you must first grasp the psychological concepts that underpin why customers say "yes" and, more crucially, why they don't.
How Customers Make Purchasing Decisions
1. The Dual Brain: Logic vs Emotion
The human brain functions at two levels: logical and

emotional. The rational brain (or System 2, as characterized by psychologist Daniel Kahneman) analyses facts, evaluates pros and disadvantages, and makes intentional choices. However, the emotional brain (System 1) is quicker, more instinctual, and often determines the ultimate decision.

While customers may feel their judgments are entirely rational, research indicates that emotions play an important impact. Even in technical or high-stakes sectors, emotions like trust, anxiety, excitement, or relief have a strong effect on results. A customer may rationalize a decision based on reasoning, but the underlying motivation is frequently how they feel about you, your competence, and the solution you provide.

As an expert, you need to appeal to both systems. Provide strong facts and statistics for the logical brain, but do not overlook the emotional connection. Stories, empathy, and reassurance may all produce great emotional resonance, tipping the scales in your favor.

2. The Need for Clarity

Clients want clarification. In a world full of information, ambiguity is the enemy of decision-making. If customers don't grasp what you're giving, how it helps them, or how it addresses their unique issue, they'll be hesitant—or worse, leave.

This is where the expert's function as a guide is crucial. Simplify complicated topics. Speak in words that your customer understands. Show them the road from their issue to your answer in a manner that is rational and attainable.

3. Risk and loss aversion.

Clients are inherently afraid of dangers, and this apprehension is heightened when making choices using knowledge they do not completely understand. They are afraid of squandering time, and money, or making a bad decision that would reflect negatively on them. Loss aversion is a psychological term that refers to the inclination to avoid losses rather than seek equal rewards.

As an expert, you must address these concerns proactively. Emphasize the safety and security of your solution. Provide examples of previous triumphs and testimonials. Assure them that their faith in you is not a risk, but rather a measured move towards resolution.

4. Social Proof and Authority.

Clients often seek others for affirmation. This is the social proof principle: when individuals are hesitant, they look to the experiences of others to guide their judgments. Authority also matters; customers are more inclined to believe an expert who has been recognized, accredited, or recommended by trustworthy sources.

Demonstrate your authority by credentials, articles, or thought leadership. Simultaneously, use social proof by sharing customer tales, case studies, or testimonials to illustrate your influence. These tools not only demonstrate your competence but also comfort them that others have benefitted from your advice.

The Function of Trust and Emotional Intelligence

1. Trust as the Foundation for Decision-Making

Trust is the unseen thread that connects everything. Without it, no amount of knowledge or persuasion will suffice. Consistency, honesty, and empathy are essential for building trust. Clients must trust in both your ability and your objectives.

Building trust takes more than just technical understanding. It entails showing up sincerely, keeping commitments, and prioritizing the client's requirements before your own. It's about being honest, even if the reality is difficult, and proving that you value the connection above the sale.

2. Emotional Intelligence, the Expert's Secret Weapon

Emotional intelligence (EI) is the capacity to recognize, interpret, and control your own and others' emotions. It's an important ability in selling knowledge because it allows you to traverse the emotional world of decision-making.

Empathy: Understand your client's worries, desires, and motives. Listen actively and validate their emotions.

Self-awareness: Be conscious of how your tone, body language, and words influence the customer. Don't come out as arrogant or contemptuous.

Adaptability: Tailor your approach to the client's emotional state and communication style. A high-energy pitch may appeal to one customer but overwhelm another.

EI enables you to connect with your customers on a deeper level, making them feel heard, appreciated, and valued. This emotional connection often determines their decision to collaborate with you.

3. The Trust and Emotion Loop

Trust and emotions do not exist in isolation; they interact in a continuous cycle. When a customer trusts you, they are more willing to share their actual problems and feelings. This transparency enables you to better answer their requirements, which strengthens their trust. In contrast, a lack of trust generates emotional boundaries that are difficult to overcome.

Your ability to handle this loop is crucial. Approach each conversation with empathy and a genuine want to assist. These modest acts of kindness and compassion add up over time, laying the groundwork for long-term partnerships.

Bring It All Together

To properly comprehend the psychology of decision-making, you must take a comprehensive approach.

Balance reasoning with emotion. Present a well-thought-out argument while developing an emotional connection.

Simplify the road ahead. Help customers gain confidence and clarity regarding their future moves.

Address your worries and hazards. Be proactive in minimizing uncertainty.

Utilise social proof and authority. Provide real-world examples and endorsements to boost your credibility.

Develop trust via emotional intelligence. Listen, adapt, and answer to customers with real concern.

When you combine these factors, you create a setting in which clients feel comfortable, supported, and prepared to make choices. Selling expertise is not about selling solutions; it is about leading customers through the decision-making process with empathy, insight, and clarity.

Understanding the psychology of client decision-making allows you to convert your talks into compelling, trust-building encounters that lead to long-term relationships.

From Selling to Guiding

The classic image of selling is often connected with

persuasion, pressure, and performance. It's all about promoting a product or service, closing the sale, and moving on to the next customer. However, this strategy is essentially faulty when it comes to marketing knowledge. Experts don't only offer solutions; they also sell trust, insight, and the promise of change.

To succeed, change your approach from selling to guiding. Instead of attempting to persuade them to choose you, assist them in identifying their requirements, explain their objectives, and show how your skills may help them succeed. This collaborative method is not only more successful but also more honest and satisfying.

Selling is a collaborative process.

1. Redefining the Role of the Expert

In conventional sales, the seller often portrays himself as the star of the show. They control the debate by highlighting their qualifications, accomplishments, and solutions. However, in the domain of knowledge, this strategy might backfire. Clients don't need a star; they need a guide.

A guide does not overshadow the customer. Instead, they encourage the customer to take center stage. You must assist them in navigating their obstacles, identifying opportunities, and making educated choices. When you approach the sales process as a collaborative effort, you move the emphasis from "me" to "we," resulting in a relationship that seems more like a shared experience than a transaction.

2. Co-creating Solutions

Collaboration is working with the customer to co-create solutions rather than delivering pre-packaged answers. This requires curiosity, flexibility, and a willingness to let go of preconceived ideas.

Co-creation starts with a thorough awareness of the client's reality. What are their sore spots? What are their aspirations? What hurdles do they face? By including the client in the discovery process, you show respect for their unique viewpoint and promote a feeling of ownership in the solution.

As the debate progresses, your knowledge becomes a tool for developing ideas, rather than dictating them. You give frameworks, ideas, and options, but the ultimate answer comes from collaborative investigation. This collaborative approach not only fosters confidence but also assures that the customer is genuinely involved in the results.

3. Prioritising Partnership Over Persuasion

Traditional sales might seem combative, with one side winning and the other compromising. However, when you present yourself as a guide, the dynamic changes to one of collaboration. You and the customer are on the same page, working towards the same objective.

This collaborative mentality is particularly helpful when making difficult or high-stakes choices. Clients do not want to be forced; they want to feel supported. They do not want to be sold; rather, they want to be understood. By taking on a leading position, you may create an atmosphere in which clients feel comfortable, respected, and empowered to make choices at their speed.

The Art of Questioning Instead of Answering

1. Why Do Questions Matter?

The questions you pose as an expert are significantly more compelling than the answers you provide. Why? Because inquiries encourage clients to think deeply, ponder on their circumstances, and discover previously unconsidered ideas. They transfer the emphasis from your knowledge to the client's demands, fostering a feeling of involvement and cooperation.

Questions also exhibit humility and curiosity, two attributes that foster trust. Instead of coming off as someone who professes to know everything, you present yourself as someone who sincerely wants to learn and assist.

2. What Types of Questions to Ask

Not all questions are created equally. To properly advise the customer, you must ask the correct questions at the appropriate moment.

Open-ended questions urge the customer to expand and provide additional information. Examples include: "What challenges are you currently facing in this area?"

Clarifying Questions: These allow you to go deeper and discover underlying difficulties. One example is: "Can you tell me more about why that's been difficult?"

Visionary Questions: These invite the customer to reflect on their aims and ambitions. Let's say: "What would success look like for you in this situation?"

Prioritizing Questions: These assist the customer in concentrating on what is most important. Let's say: "Which of these issues feels most urgent to address right now?"

Using a combination of these questions, you may lead the client through a journey of discovery and understanding.

3. Listening With Intent

Asking questions is just half of the equation; the other half is listening—truly listening. Too frequently, salesmen use inquiries to direct the discussion towards their solution. However, as a guide, your objective is to listen intently and curiously, with no preconceived notions or intentions.

When you listen carefully, you may pick up on details that might otherwise be missed. You hear not just the words, but also the emotions, anxieties, and motives that drive them. This degree of information enables you to modify your replies and solutions in a personalized manner.

4. Allowing the client to arrive at their answers.

One of the most significant parts of asking questions is that it enables the client to reach their conclusions. When customers believe they have reached their own decision, they are far more inclined to trust and adhere to it.

This does not imply that you suppress your knowledge; rather, you utilize it wisely. Instead of providing straight answers, you provide suggestions and frameworks to enable the customer to connect the connections. This strategy not only fosters trust but also strengthens your reputation as a thoughtful, collaborative partner.

Mental shift

Shifting from selling to coaching takes more than simply new approaches; it necessitates a fundamental shift in mentality. You must abandon the assumption that your job is to persuade and instead embrace the idea that you must empower.

This mentality adjustment offers significant advantages. It helps the sales process seem more natural and consistent with your ideals. It fosters closer ties with customers. And it results in greater outcomes—not just for you, but also for those you serve.

When you view selling as a guide, you go beyond transactions. You build trust. You instill confidence. And you create long-term relationships based on mutual respect and success.

This is the art of selling expertise: not by pushing solutions, but by assisting customers in discovering, understanding, and accepting the value you provide.

Part 2: The Four Conversations

Conversation 1: Discovery

The Discovery Conversation is the first step in establishing a meaningful client connection. It serves as the basis for developing trust, understanding, and cooperation. Consider it the time when you, the expert, go from selling to investigating with empathy. During this period, you are not pushing solutions or demonstrating credentials. Instead, you delve deeply into the client's environment, trying to understand their wants, issues, and goals.

When done correctly, the Discovery Conversation alters the relationship between you and the customer. It demonstrates that you are there to serve them, not simply sell them something. It establishes you as a partner who is attentive enough to listen and astute enough to ask the appropriate questions. Identifying the client's needs and pain points

1. The Power of Context.

Every customer has a narrative, and their wants and pain areas are chapters in it. To properly appreciate what they need, you must first grasp the context:

What industry are they in?

What role do they play in their organization?

What are the larger issues that their organization or market is facing?

Context provides significance to the client's challenges. Without it, their pain locations may seem superficial or isolated. However, given context, you can connect the dots between their problems and the solutions you provide.

For example, a customer may express concern about staff engagement. This seems to be a widespread problem. However, with further background, you could learn that they work in a highly competitive business where keeping talent is vital to survival. This transforms the discussion from a general issue to an urgent, high-stakes situation.

2. Identifying Explicit and Implicit Needs

Clients often express specific needs—things they know they need assistance with. However, the true value of the Discovery Conversation resides in revealing their latent needs—things people may not even be aware of are difficulties.

For example, a customer may state that they want improved reporting tools to monitor performance. This is a clear necessity. However, with diligent probing, you may discover an underlying need: their team lacks clarity regarding strategic objectives, making performance tracking ineffective. By addressing both explicit and implicit demands, you establish yourself as a genuine issue solution.

3. The Emotional Level of Pain Points

Every pain location has an emotional component in addition to its surface-level issues. This is where the client's anxieties, frustrations, and wishes are. Understanding these emotions is important since choices, particularly high-stakes ones, are often motivated by feelings rather than reasoning.

Consider a customer who is experiencing diminishing sales. On the surface, this seems to be a business challenge. But go further, and you may discover that the customer feels personally accountable for the drop, or that they are concerned about losing credibility with their team. Addressing these emotional layers not only allows you to adapt your solution but also fosters a stronger relationship with the customer.

Tips for Active Listening

Active listening is the foundation of the Discovery Conversation. It's more than simply hearing words; it's about genuinely comprehending what the client is saying—and not saying.

1. Elements of Active Listening

Focus Fully on the customer: Remove any distractions and offer the customer your entire attention. This demonstrates respect and promotes trust.

Listen to Understand, Not Respond: Resist the urge to create your answer as the customer speaks. Your job is to comprehend, not to provide answers.

Observe Nonverbal Cues: Pay attention to the client's tone, body language, and facial expression. These often disclose more than just words.

Reflect and Clarify: Paraphrase what the customer has stated to ensure you understand. For example, "It sounds like you're dissatisfied with the current process because it's reducing your team's productivity." Is that correct?

Stay Curious: Approach the discussion with genuine interest. Ask follow-up questions to delve further into the client's ideas and emotions.

2. The Role of Silence

Silence may be an effective technique in active listening. After asking a question, avoid the temptation to fill the quiet. Allow the customer to ponder and reply. Often, the most significant discoveries come from just waiting.

3. Managing your biases

As an expert, you most certainly have predetermined notions about what the client's issue is and how to resolve it. While these instincts might be useful, they can also impede your capacity to fully listen. Approach each Discovery

Conversation with an open mind and leave aside preconceptions until you have all of the facts.

The Art of Open-ended Questioning

Open-ended inquiries are the heart of the Discovery Conversation. They inspire the customer to disclose more, think more deeply, and uncover ideas they may not have considered before.

1. The characteristics of great questions.

An excellent question is broad enough to stimulate investigation while being detailed enough to keep the discussion on track. For instance, "What's your biggest challenge right now?"

Nonjudgmental: Avoid asking inquiries that may make the client feel defensive. Substitute: "Why haven't you solved this problem yet?" resolve "What obstacles have been making this problem difficult to address?"

Future-oriented: Encourage the customer to consider their ambitions and aspirations. Examples include: "If this issue were resolved, what would success look like for you?"

2. Examples of Powerful Questions

"What's keeping you up at night when it comes to this issue?"

"Can you walk me through how this problem impacts your day-to-day operations?"

"How have you tried to address this challenge in the past, and what were the results?"

"What would it mean for your team if we could solve this?"

"What's holding you back from tackling this issue right now?"

3. Building on Responses.

The Discovery Conversation is not a list of questions; it is a dynamic conversation. When the customer replies, let their responses influence your next inquiry. For example:

The client stated: "We've been struggling with communication between departments."

You say, "That's fascinating. Can you provide an example of how that breakdown impacted your projects?"

This technique demonstrates that you are actively interested and allows the discussion to flow smoothly.

Mastering the Discovery Conversation.

When done correctly, the Discovery Conversation has numerous important outcomes:

It allows you to have a comprehensive understanding of the client's requirements, pain areas, and objectives.

It exhibits empathy, curiosity, and a desire to discover the best answer.

It establishes you as a trustworthy counselor rather than a salesman.

But, more crucially, it sets the tone for the whole partnership. A good Discovery Conversation establishes the foundation for trust, cooperation, and mutual success.

As you improve your active listening and open-ended asking abilities, you'll discover that the Discovery Conversation is more than simply a sales process step—it's a powerful tool for making meaningful connections and achieving effective outcomes.

Conversation 2: Insight

After successfully navigating the Discovery Conversation, the Insight Conversation is the next essential step. This is when your knowledge starts to take center stage, but not in the manner you may expect. The idea here is not to overwhelm the customer with information, jargon, or great credentials. Instead, integrate your knowledge into meaningful, practical insights that are directly relevant to the client's unique goals and issues.

The Insight Conversation allows you to communicate value in a manner that seems natural, customized, and compelling. It is about bridging the gap between the client's pain areas and the answers you provide—without overwhelming them with information.

Providing value without overloading information.

1. The dangers of information overload

Experts often confront a dilemma: they want to demonstrate their expertise, yet they risk overloading the customer with too much information. This leads to two outcomes:

The customer closes down: They may be confused or

afraid, particularly if they lack the same degree of technical ability.

The core message is buried: In your attempt to explain everything, the customer may struggle to understand what is genuinely important.

To prevent these issues, prioritize curation. Your goal is not to share everything you know, but to share the relevant information—the insights that are most important to the client.

2. Tailoring Insights for the Client's Needs

Each customer is unique, and the insights you give should reflect this. This is when your efforts in the Discovery Conversation pay off. Use the data you've acquired to create insights that are:

Relevant: Address the client's unique pain issues and aspirations.

Contextualized: Tailor your findings to the client's specific position or industry.

Prioritized: Emphasise the issues that are most important or valuable to the client.

For example, instead of stating, "We offer comprehensive training programs," you may respond by adding, "Based on what you've shared about your team's struggles with onboarding, I believe a tailored training program focused on quick wins in the first 90 days could significantly boost retention and productivity."

3. Keeping it simple and actionable

The most effective insights are those that the client can easily understand and apply. Use simple, direct language and avoid unnecessary jargon. Whenever possible, divide complex ideas into manageable chunks and link them to measurable outcomes.

Instead of delving into the technical specifics of a new procedure, you may remark, "This change would save your team 10 hours per week, freeing them up to focus on strategic initiatives rather than repetitive tasks."

How to present your expertise as a solution.

1. Positioning Yourself as a Problem Solver

The Insight Conversation is not about you; it is about the customer. While it is crucial to emphasize your experience, the emphasis should always be on how that knowledge translates into solutions to the client's problems.

To do this, present your ideas as solutions to the client's most urgent issues. For example:

The client's concern: "We're struggling to scale operations without adding significant costs."

Your insight: "One solution is to optimize your workflow through automation. For example, we've helped comparable businesses decrease manual activities by 40%, allowing them to grow without adding personnel."

This approach subtly demonstrates your expertise while keeping the conversation centered on the client's needs.

2. Connecting Expertise to Outcomes

Clients care less about how you accomplish what you do and more about what it will achieve for them. Always bring your knowledge back to quantifiable or meaningful results.

For example, instead of stating, "I specialize in data analytics," you may add, "By analyzing your customer data, I can help you identify key trends that will inform more targeted marketing strategies, ultimately increasing your conversion rates."

This framing changes the attention from your skill set to the client's desired goals, making your knowledge seem more concrete and meaningful.

3. Using Stories and Examples

Stories are one of the most effective tools in the Insight Conversation. They make abstract concepts tangible, establish credibility, and establish an emotional connection with the customer.

When telling a narrative, emphasis on:

The issue: What hurdle did the prior customer face?

The solution: How did your knowledge contribute to overcoming the challenge?

The outcome: What quantifiable or meaningful outcomes were obtained?

For example:

"A retail customer I dealt with was having inventory

management issues, which resulted in frequent stock outs. They increased sales by $500,000 after installing a predictive analytics system suited to business requirements and reducing stock outs by 25% in the first quarter.

This method not only demonstrates your competence but also helps the customer to see comparable outcomes for themselves.

Balancing Confidence and Collaboration

1. Avoiding the "Expert Knows Best" Trap

While it is crucial to show confidence, avoid coming off as prescriptive or dismissive of the client's ideas. Remember that this is a collaborative effort. The customer should feel like an active collaborator in developing the solution, rather than a passive beneficiary of your skills.

Instead of stating, "This is what you need to do," you may say, "Based on what we've discussed, here's a strategy that I believe will work well." How does it fit with your vision?"

This minor alteration in terminology promotes debate and strengthens the feeling of collaboration.

2. Listening for feedback and making adjustments

Even in the Insight Conversation, listening is crucial. Pay attention to the client's responses, both vocal and nonverbal, and be ready to modify your approach depending on their input.

For example, if the customer is apprehensive about a certain proposal, avoid pushing it. Instead, consider their concerns: "I saw some reluctance at this time. Is there anything in particular you're concerned about?"

This not only helps you improve your ideas, but it also shows that you are prepared to change and participate.

Emotional Component of Insight

Insights are more than simply facts and reasoning; they also include emotion. To fully engage with the customer, your insights must connect with their inner motivations, anxieties, and goals.

For example, if a customer is concerned about losing market share, your advice might not only address the tactical issues of restoring competitiveness but also reassure them that they have the resources and support they need to succeed. This emotional comfort may be as effective as the actual answer.

Mastering the Insight Conversation.

The Insight Conversation is a careful balancing act. You must display your knowledge without overwhelming the customer, provide unique solutions without being too prescriptive, and strike a balance between confidence and cooperation.

When done properly, this conversation:

Positions you as a trustworthy counselor who knows the client's specific issues.

Demonstrate how your knowledge translates into useful, practical solutions.

Creates enthusiasm and trust in the customer, paving the way for the next phase of the partnership.

By focussing on providing value, skilfully presenting your knowledge, and keeping a collaborative tone, you guarantee that the Insight Conversation is transformational rather than just informational. It's the point at which your knowledge transforms from abstract to actionable, confirming your position as the guide who will lead the customer to success.

Conversation 3: Partnership

The Partnership Conversation is when the magic occurs. It is the point at which you and the customer cease to be different entities—the expert and the seeker—and instead become a team bound by a common goal. This is not a transactional talk; rather, it is a collaborative process that prioritizes trust, alignment, and co-creation.

You've already discovered the client's requirements and pain areas in the Discovery Conversation and offered useful thoughts in the Insight Conversation. The Partnership Conversation is going ahead together. It's where ideas become practical goals and trust grows into a strong basis for a professional partnership.

Co-creating a Path Forward

1. Switching from "Expert Mode" to "Collaborator Mode."

The key to co-creating a route ahead is to shift from dictation to collaboration. This does not imply forsaking your knowledge; rather, it means utilizing it as a tool to help the customer. Instead of offering a hard answer, include the customer in the process of developing it.

For example:

Instead of declaring, "Here's what we're going to do," offer, "Based on our discussions, I have a few ideas on how we can approach this." Let us explore them together and modify them depending on your feedback."

This strategy guarantees that the customer feels ownership of the solution, which boosts buy-in and sets the stage for a fruitful collaboration.

2. Mapping Out the Steps Together

Clarity and organization are essential when co-creating a strategy. Begin by describing the broad strokes of the course ahead, then work with the customer to fill in the specifics. Define your objectives: what does success look like? What are your immediate and long-term goals?

Identify key milestones: What are the most important stages along the way?

Assign Roles and Responsibilities: Who is going to do what? How will you collaborate to attain the goals? For example, you may remark, "To meet your objective of boosting customer retention by 20%, we'll need to concentrate on three major areas: improving client onboarding, upgrading the loyalty program, and introducing stronger follow-up techniques. How do these areas relate to your priorities?

This collaborative approach fosters congruence while also establishing clear expectations for both sides.

3. Balancing Structure and Flexibility.

While having a clear strategy is vital, so is being adaptable. The client's requirements and circumstances may change, and the partnership must be flexible enough to adjust.

Recognize this up front: "This is our beginning position, but as we go ahead, we'll constantly analyze and adapt depending on what we learn. Does that technique work for you?

This reassures the customer that you are devoted to their achievement rather than just following a script.

Creating Trust via Alignment and Collaboration

1. Aligning goals and values.

True collaboration entails more than just agreeing on the "what"; it also requires agreement on the "why." Take the time to grasp the client's overall vision and values, and ensure that your approach is consistent with them.

For example, if the customer values sustainability, ensure that your suggested solutions reflect this. Explicitly relate your strategy to their principles: "Since sustainability is a core value for your organization, we'll ensure that our recommendations not only address your current challenges but also support your long-term commitment to environmental responsibility."

This congruence fosters trust by demonstrating to the customer that you are not just addressing their issues, but also supporting their goal.

2. Establishing a Safe Space for Feedback

Trust flourishes in an atmosphere where the customer feels comfortable sharing their thoughts, problems, and ideas. Encourage this climate by aggressively seeking input and reacting with transparency and respect.

For example:

After presenting a concept, ask, "How does this resonate with you?". Is there anything you would want to change or add?

If the customer shows doubt, address it without becoming defensive: "I understand your worry regarding the timeframe. Let's talk about how we may modify it to better suit your requirements."

By respecting the client's contribution, you promote the idea of collaboration and guarantee that the final plan seems shared.

3. Showing Commitment via Action.

Trust is developed by deeds, not just words. To demonstrate

your dedication to the collaboration, you can:
Following through on commitments.
Proactively tackling difficulties or developments.
Communicating openly about progress, failures, and modifications.
For example, if you pledge to give a thorough proposal by a specific date, ensure that it is delivered on time—or, if unavoidable delays occur, notify them quickly and explain why.

Turning Collaboration Into Momentum

1. Small wins to boost confidence.

Small victories may have a significant influence on a relationship in its early stages. Determine short-term, attainable objectives that indicate success and boost trust in the collaboration.
For example, "Before we begin full implementation, let's start

with a pilot project." This will provide us with useful information and enable us to make necessary modifications before scaling up."

These tiny victories build momentum and strengthen the client's conviction in the benefits of working with you.

2. Consistent check-ins to ensure alignment.

Partnerships need constant communication to keep on track and resolve any emergent issues. Set a schedule for frequent check-ins, whether via formal meetings or casual updates.

During the check-ins:

Evaluate progress towards objectives.

Celebrate accomplishments.

Address any issues or make any necessary modifications.

For example: "Now that we've finished the first phase, let's go over the findings and talk about what's next. Are there any changes you'd want to make before we proceed?"

These check-ins keep the collaboration active and responsive, ensuring that it continues to deliver value.

The Emotional Centre of Partnership

Beyond the technical aspects of co-creating a route ahead, the Partnership Conversation includes an emotional component. This is when trust grows and the connection transitions from professional to personal.

1. Empathy as a bridge.

Empathy is the cornerstone of every successful connection. Demonstrate to the customer that you not only understand their issues but really care about their achievement. This might be going the additional mile to handle an issue or just listening when they need to vent.

For example: "I can see this assignment is daunting

considering everything else on your plate. Let's talk about how we can make this procedure as smooth as possible for you."

2. Celebrating the client's vision.

Clients want to believe that their aims and desires are important. Celebrate their vision and reiterate your commitment to assisting them in making it a reality.

For example: "Your commitment to provide a better customer experience is inspirational. I am thrilled to collaborate with you to make that idea a reality."

This kind of emotional affirmation reinforces the alliance and keeps the customer engaged.

Mastering the Partnership Conversation.

The Partnership Conversation is when connections are consolidated, plans are put into action, and trust is established. It's more than simply generating a road map; it's about instilling a shared sense of purpose and a commitment to achieve it together.

When done properly, this conversation:

Maintains alignment with objectives, beliefs, and expectations.

Encourages collaborative, trust-based relationships.

Creates the foundation for a successful and rewarding collaboration.

By focussing on co-creation, alignment, and emotional connection, you can change the client relationship from a transaction to a meaningful partnership that produces value, inspires confidence, and endures over time.

Conversation 4: Commitment

The Commitment Conversation brings everything together. After setting the basis in prior talks (Discovery, Insight, and Partnership), it's time to put interest into action. This discussion represents the conclusion of the trust, alignment, and understanding you've developed with your customer.

Securing commitment does not include pressing the customer to say "yes." Instead, it's about leading them to a natural choice point where continuing seems like the clear and reasonable next step. This interaction needs subtlety, confidence, and a thorough grasp of what drives the customer to act.

Converting Interest to Action

1. Clearing the Way Forward

Before the customer can commit, they must properly comprehend what they are agreeing to. Ambiguity may lead to hesitancy, thus it's important to present a well-defined strategy that outlines the following:

The goal: What do you want to accomplish together?

What measures will be taken and when?

The predicted outcomes: What advantages or results may the customer anticipate?

For example: "After our discussions, we will launch the pilot program." This will last four weeks and will mostly concentrate on optimizing your onboarding process. We'll analyze the pilot findings and adjust the method before ramping up. Does that timetable work for you?

This degree of clarity reassures the customer that you have a solid strategy and allows them to see the way ahead.

2. Managing Hesitation and Unspoken Concerns

Even the most eager customers may have misgivings. These might be budgetary, time, or results-related uncertainties. To turn curiosity into action, you must identify and address these problems.

Encourage frank discussion of problems. Create a safe area for the customer to express any concerns. For example, "Is there anything that makes you hesitate about going forward? I want to be sure we've addressed all of your issues."

Acknowledge and validate: Demonstrate empathy by accepting that their worries are legitimate. For example, "I understand that committing to a new approach might seem hazardous, particularly when finances are short. Let's talk about ways to reduce that danger.

Provide reassurance. Provide proof or instances to counteract their fears, such as success stories or statistics.

3. Framing the action as low-risk

People are generally risk-averse, therefore lowering perceived risk might help the customer commit. Strategies include:

Start small: Offer a staged strategy that enables the customer to test the waters.

Guarantees: If necessary, provide assurances such as performance guarantees or flexible terms.

Highlighting opportunity costs: Gently remind the customer of the consequences if they do not act.

For example, "We could begin with a one-month trial period." This allows you to assess the effect before making a long-term commitment. And, since your rivals are also considering similar methods, stepping ahead now might offer you a significant edge."

Strategies to Secure Buy-In Without Being Pushy

1. Collaborative decision-making.

The Commitment Conversation should seem like a natural continuation of the Partnership Conversation, not a forced sale. Approach it as a collaborative effort.

Use inclusive language when asking, "What do you think the best next step is?"

Involve the customer in refining the plan: "Are there any changes you'd like to make before we move forward?"

This strategy strengthens the feeling of shared ownership while decreasing opposition.

2. Showing Confidence Without Pressure

Clients are more inclined to commit when they believe in

your strategy. Confidence, however, does not imply pressuring people into making a choice; rather, it entails expressing your views with clarity and conviction.

For example, "I am confident that this approach will help you achieve the results we discussed." Let us go with the first part, and I will be there to accompany you every step of the way."

This tone shows confidence without making the customer feel pressured.

3. Applying Social Proof and Case Studies

Sharing examples of previous customers who have completed comparable tasks helps boost confidence and lessen hesitancy.

For example, a client in a comparable position reported a 30% increase in customer retention after implementing this method within three months. I think we can provide comparable outcomes for you."

This form of social evidence tells the customer that your suggestions are based on demonstrated success.

Building Emotional Resonance

1. Tapping into Motivation

People base their judgments on both reasoning and emotion. To gain commitment, tie your proposal to the client's deeper motives, such as their desire to solve an urgent issue, accomplish a big objective, or make an effect.

For instance, this strategy aims to provide your staff with the necessary skills to feel empowered and confident in their job, not only to increase productivity. That kind of shift may revolutionize your whole organization."

2. Celebrating the client's vision.

Reiterate your conviction in the client's objectives and capacity to attain them. This emotional confirmation may motivate individuals to act.

For example, "Your vision for a seamless customer experience is truly inspiring." I'm looking forward to contributing to the realization of that objective. Let us take the first step together.

Handling objections gracefully
Even with the finest planning, objections might occur. The way you manage them will make or ruin the discussion.

1. Be calm and curious.
Resist the impulse to respond to criticisms instantly. Instead, try to grasp the fundamental issue. For example:

The client stated: "I'm not sure we're ready to commit right now."

You said, "I understand. Can you tell me what's making you feel that way? "Is it the timing, the approach, or something else?"

This approach shows respect and keeps the discussion open.

2. Reframe the objections as opportunities.

Once you grasp the issue, see it as an opportunity to improve the strategy. For example:

Objection: "This seems like a large investment."

Response: "I understand. Let's look at methods to stagger the implementation to spread out the investment while still making significant progress."

Closing with confidence and clarity

1. Making the Next Step Clear.

Finish the discussion with a clear call to action that seems natural and sensible. For instance, "Based on our discussions, I recommend moving forward with the implementation phase." I will send along the finalized plan and set up a launch meeting for next week. Does it work for you?

2. Strengthening the partnership.

Remind the customer that this is just the beginning of your cooperation and that you are dedicated to their success. For instance, "Moving forward is the first step in what I believe will be a successful partnership." I'll be present every step of the way to guarantee we get the outcomes you want."

The Art of Commitment Conversation

The Commitment Conversation isn't about completing a transaction; it's about building trust and turning stated objectives into tangible activities. When done properly, it:

Converts curiosity into a confident "yes."

It reinforces the collaborative attitude of the partnership.

Establishes the foundation for a successful and rewarding collaboration.

By emphasizing clarity, cooperation, and emotional connection, you can help customers make a commitment that feels appropriate for them—and for you. This last step is more than simply a transaction; it marks the start of our adventure together.

Part 3: Applying the Model

Adapting the Four Conversations to Different Contexts

The Four Conversations paradigm (Discovery, Insight, Partnership, and Commitment) provides a diverse method of marketing knowledge. However, its actual strength comes from its versatility. Different sectors, clientele, and circumstances need varied responses. By customizing the approach to individual situations, experts may increase its efficacy and build stronger relationships with their customers.

Let's look at how to adapt the Four Conversations to different businesses and customer types, leaving no stone untouched on this road to customization.

Tailoring for Different Industries

Each sector has its issues, lingo, and client expectations. Customizing the Four Conversations to meet industry standards provides relevance and resonance.

1. Professional Services (law, accounting, and consulting)

Clients often seek professional advice to help them negotiate complicated, high-stakes challenges. Here's how to adjust.

Discovery: Determine the client's particular pain areas, such as regulatory compliance, risk management, or financial wellness. Ask questions that will disclose the underlying consequences of these difficulties.

Insight: Discuss your previous experience in comparable situations. Provide useful information without overwhelming the customer with technical jargon. For example, in a legal setting, explain how a precedent pertains to their circumstance.

Partnership: Encourage cooperation by including the customer in strategy formulation. In consulting, this might include co-creating a path for organizational transformation.

Commitment: Respond to the high stakes by offering reassurances. Offer gradual techniques or promises to lessen perceived risk.

2. Technology & SaaS

Technology customers often encounter quickly changing difficulties and seek new solutions. The Four Conversations may be modified to emphasize agility and forward-thinking:

Discovery: Investigate the client's operational obstacles, such as inefficiencies or scalability issues. Use diagnostic techniques to find hidden pain spots.

Insight: Offer forward-thinking ideas based on industry trends. Explain, for example, how using a certain technology can help to future-proof their business.

Partnership: Demonstrate your commitment to long-term support by providing training, onboarding, and periodic updates.

Commitment: Highlight your solution's concrete ROI, such as cost savings or higher productivity. Provide demonstrations or trial initiatives to boost confidence.

3. Creative industries (marketing, design, and media)

Clients in the creative sectors place a high emphasis on innovation and emotional connection. Use the Four Conversations to inspire and connect:

Discovery: Investigate the client's vision, brand identity, and intended audience. Ask open-ended inquiries to discover their creative goals.

Insight: Provide instances of comparable innovative techniques that have produced success. Use graphics or narrative to make your thoughts more engaging.

Partnership: Prioritise co-creation. For example, in a design project, engage the customer in brainstorming sessions or mood board creation.

Commitment: Focus on the project's emotional effect. Paint a realistic picture of how your efforts will alter their brand.

Adapting for Different Client Types

Clients differ not just by industry, but also by position, personality, and decision-making style. Tailoring the Four Conversations to specific customer types improves their efficacy.

1. Analytical clients.

Data and logic are the top priorities for analytical customers. They are detail-oriented and may demand extensive proof before making conclusions.

Ask specific, fact-based inquiries to discover their issues. Example: "What metrics are you currently tracking, and where are the gaps?"

Insight: Provide data-driven insights, such as market

analyses or case studies. Use charts or graphs to demonstrate your ideas.

Partnership: Develop a defined strategy with specific goals and quantifiable results. Analytical customers place a high importance on predictability.

Commitment: Provide proof to address any possible concerns. Provide extensive documentation or simulations to boost trust.

2. Clients who prioritize relationship-building

Clients who value relationships put trust and emotional connection first. They are likely to cherish the cooperation just as much as the results.

Discovery: Establish rapport by expressing genuine interest in their aspirations and ideals. Use empathic listening to discover their needs.

Insight: Share personal tales or instances that evoke

emotion. For example, discuss how your efforts positively influenced another customer.

Collaboration and adaptability are key components of a partnership. Reassure them that you are willing to adjust as their requirements change.

Commitment: Present the choice as a joint step towards a shared objective. Use affirmative words, such as "Together, we can make this happen."

3. Time-Constrained Decision Makers

Busy executives and leaders place a high emphasis on efficiency. They want precise, actionable data to make speedy judgments.

Discovery: Concentrate on high-impact queries that get to the point. Let's say: "What's the most pressing challenge you're facing right now?"

Insight: Summarise essential information in a concise, executive-friendly way.

Present solutions in the form of bullet points or a one-page summary.

Partnership: Propose efficient procedures that value their time. Offer to do as much of the legwork as feasible.

Commitment: Make a concise, uncomplicated call to action. For example, "Here is a one-page outline of the next steps." Let us plan a brief follow-up to finalize."

Context-specific Scenarios

Certain situations need distinct modifications of the Four Conversations. Let us consider some examples:

1. Startups & Entrepreneurs

Startups often operate under high-pressure, resource-constrained conditions. Adapting to their requirements requires quickness and innovation.

Discovery: Concentrate on their vision and development issues. Ask questions such as, "What's the biggest impediment to scaling your business?"

Insight: Offer realistic, low-cost solutions that are appropriate for their stage of development. Share techniques or tricks that show immediate results.

Partnership: Demonstrate a grasp of their entrepreneurial path. Position yourself as a flexible and hands-on collaborator.

Commitment: Emphasise quickness and flexibility. Provide flexible terms or phased programs to fit their changing surroundings.

2. Established Enterprises

Large organizations often use complicated decision-making procedures and layers of bureaucracy. Use the Four Conversations to navigate these complexities:

Discovery: Consult with a variety of stakeholders to get insight into different points of view. To acquire insights, hold seminars, or administer surveys.

Insight: Present scalable solutions that are consistent with the organization's strategic objectives. Use terminology that is relevant to company aims, such as "efficiency" or "competitive advantage."

Partnership: Involve important players in the planning process to help achieve agreement.

Commitment: Provide a thorough implementation plan that proves your ability to manage complex projects.

Adapting To Cultural Differences

Cultural variations may have a big influence on how customers react to the Four Conversations. Being culturally aware increases the efficacy of your approach.

Be cognizant of communication styles. In certain cultures, consumers may choose to avoid conflict by asking indirect queries.

Insight: Tailor your presentation approach to reflect cultural standards. For example, certain cultures value narrative, whilst others favor data-driven methods.

Respect hierarchical structures. In societies with high power dynamics, prioritize developing connections with decision-makers.

Commitment: Be mindful of the decision-making timetable. Decisions in certain cultures may take longer because of the emphasis on consensus-building.

The Four Conversations model's strength is its versatility. Create a more personalized and powerful experience by adapting each interaction to the specific demands of diverse businesses, customers, and circumstances. This customization not only improves your capacity to market knowledge, but also strengthens your connections, fosters trust, and generates long-term benefits.

In a world where no two customers or circumstances are the same, the capacity to adapt is your most important asset. The Four Conversations framework offers structure; but, your adaptation brings it to life.

Overcoming Objections and Challenges: Handling Resistance and Hesitation Effectively

Resistance and hesitancy are unavoidable components of every path toward change, success, or innovation. Whether you're selling a product, promoting an idea, developing a relationship, or pursuing personal progress, objections and hurdles are unavoidable. The trick is to comprehend them, face them front on, and turn barriers into possibilities.

1. Understanding the Roots of Objections.

Fear, uncertainty, and a lack of knowledge are common sources of objections. Before delving into techniques to overcome them, it is essential to recognize their underlying causes:

Fear of Change: Change upsets the existing quo and brings the unknown to light. People naturally resist because they feel safer in their comfortable surroundings.

Lack of Information: When individuals don't have enough information, they may make assumptions, which might lead to skepticism.

Negative prior experiences might lead to prejudice against

prospects, even if they vary from the previous case.

Perceived Risks: People may hesitate when they believe possible risks—whether financial, emotional, or social—outweigh the rewards.

2. The Power of Empathy.

Empathy is your most effective weapon for overcoming opposition. When someone hesitates or raises an issue, take a step back and imagine yourself in their position.

Listen Actively: Listening is more than simply hearing words; it is also about comprehending feelings and worries. Allow individuals to voice their doubts freely and without interruption.

Validate Their Feelings: Demonstrate understanding by recognizing their worries. A remark like, "I can understand why you'd feel that way," might dispel defensiveness and open the door to discourse.

3. Strategies to Overcome Objections

A. Provide clarity.

Frequently, hesitancy originates from a lack of precise information. When you foresee objections, aggressively address them with:

Facts and Data: Back up your claims with reliable data. Facts may assist in overcoming emotional reluctance.

Personal tales or customer testimonials might show how others overcome similar uncertainties to profit from the choice.

Simplified Explanations: Avoid jargon and overly complex explanations. Speak clearly and directly.

B. Reframe the Perspective.

Help people see the situation from a different perspective:

Focus on the Benefits: Highlight the positive outcomes and value they will receive. Change the emphasis from costs or risks to benefits and opportunities.

Turn Negatives Into Positives: For example, if someone says, "This is too expensive," point out the long-term savings or value they will receive.

C. Build Trust

Trust is the foundation of all decision-making processes. To build it:

Credibility: Showcase your expertise and dependability with credentials, experience, or a proven track record.

Be Transparent: Being open about challenges or limitations can help you gain credibility faster than making empty promises.

Offer Guarantees: A satisfaction guarantee or trial period can reduce perceived risk and persuade hesitant individuals to proceed.

D. Use the Power of Questions.

Ask open-ended questions to elicit hidden concerns and guide the conversation:

"What's holding you back from moving forward?"

"What would need to happen for you to feel comfortable taking this step?"

"How does this align with your goals or needs?"

These questions foster debate and might help highlight particular concerns.

4. Handling Emotional Resistance

Sometimes arguments are more emotional than rational. These demand a gentle touch:

Diffuse Tension: Stay cool and controlled, even if the other person gets upset. Your calm might assist bring them back to a sensible condition.

Offer Reassurance: Provide emotional support by demonstrating that you care about their well-being.

5. Turning Challenges into Opportunities

Every criticism offers a chance to improve your argument, develop your strategy, and expand connections. Consider objections as feedback rather than obstacles:

Refine Your Offer: Objections often highlight gaps in your offer or communication. Use them to make improvements.

Strengthen Relationships: Addressing challenges effectively can foster respect and trust, making the relationship more robust.

6. The Role of Persistence

Overcoming objections isn't always about a single conversation. Persistence, when done politely, may make all the difference:

Follow-Up: Sometimes, people need time to process information or weigh their options. A thoughtful follow-up shows commitment.

Stay Patient: Don't pressure or rush people into decisions. Give them space while remaining available for further discussions.

7. The Art of Adaptation

Not all objections will have a one-size-fits-all solution. Adaptability is crucial:

Tailor Your Approach: Understand the individual or audience you're dealing with and adapt your strategy to their unique needs and concerns.

Stay Open to Feedback: If your initial attempts do not resonate, be willing to change your approach.

8. Be prepared for the unexpected.

Some objections may take you off guard. Being ready is half the battle:

Anticipate Common Challenges: Make a list of possible objections and prepare responses to each one.

Role-playing: Hold mock conversations to practice

handling resistance effectively.

9. Psychology and Decision-Making

Understanding the psychological principles that underpin objections can help you navigate them more effectively.

Cognitive dissonance occurs when people's actions conflict with their beliefs. Help them connect their decision to their values or goals.

Loss Aversion: Emphasise what they stand to lose by not taking action, as avoiding loss is often more motivating than gaining benefits.

10. A Mindset for Success

Finally, approach objections and challenges with the right mindset:

Embrace Challenges: View resistance as a chance to develop, learn, and perfect your talents.

Stay Positive: A positive attitude may transform the

tone of the discussion and instill confidence in others.

Celebrate Tiny Wins: Every tiny stride forward is something worth celebrating.

Overcoming objections and dealing with resistance is both an art and a science. It requires a combination of empathy, strategy, adaptability, and perseverance. By recognizing the fundamental reasons for reluctance, listening intently, addressing concerns wisely, and keeping an attitude of progress, you can negotiate even the greatest problems and turn resistance into chances for connection, growth, and achievement.

Integrating Technology into the Process: Leveraging Digital Tools for Expert-Client Conversations

In today's linked world, technology is more than a convenience; it is a catalyst for change. The internet world has transformed expert-client exchanges in coaching, consulting, and other professional settings. The appropriate technologies may help you improve communication, simplify procedures, and create a dynamic atmosphere that promotes cooperation and trust. This book explains how to smoothly incorporate technology into expert-client interactions to make them more interesting, efficient, and powerful.

1. A New Era of Expert-Client Interaction

While traditional face-to-face meetings are still vital, they are no longer the sole way to have meaningful interactions. Technology has new dimensions, providing flexibility and efficiency.

Global Accessibility: Experts and clients may communicate across continents without leaving their homes.

Enhanced Engagement: Interactive technologies make sessions more interesting and productive.

Data-Driven Insights: Technology enables monitoring, analyzing, and optimizing interactions.

2. Selecting the Right Digital Tools.

The efficiency of technology integration is dependent on picking the appropriate tools. Here's a breakdown of the categories and applications:

A. Communication Platforms.

Video conferencing tools like Zoom, Microsoft Teams, and Google Meet enable real-time visual engagement, simulating in-person interactions.

Instant Messaging: Platforms such as Slack and WhatsApp provide rapid and informal avenues for continuing assistance.

Email Management Systems: Tools like Outlook and Gmail

are required for organized and professional email.

B. Collaborative and Productive Tools

Shared workspaces: Google Workspace and Microsoft 365 provide real-time document sharing and editing.

Project management tools such as Asana, Trello, and Monday.com may assist monitor progress and keep both parties on track.

Digital whiteboards, such as Miro or MURAL, may make brainstorming sessions more engaging and visible.

C. Data and Analysis

CRM systems, such as Salesforce or HubSpot, assist manage client data, monitor interactions, and analyze trends.

Survey and input Tools: Google Forms and Typeform provide organized customer input.

Performance Tracking: Tools such as Toggl Track and

Clockify track time spent on activities to improve efficiency.

D. Engagement Enhancers

Presentation tools like Canva, Prezi, and PowerPoint improve visual communication.

Interactive platforms such as Kahoot or Mentimeter may be used for quizzes, polls, and real-time audience participation.

Learning Management Systems (LMS): Platforms such as Teachable and Thinkific enable professionals to develop and share course content.

3. The Power of Personalisation Through Technology.

Digital technologies allow professionals to adjust their services to unique customer demands, resulting in a personalized experience.

Customized Dashboards: Tools like Notion and Airtable enable you to create personalized client dashboards that monitor progress, objectives, and milestones.

Automated Scheduling: Calendly or Acuity simplifies appointment scheduling by removing back-and-forth emails.

AI-Powered Insights: AI technologies such as ChatGPT and Jasper provide personalized suggestions, reducing time and enhancing accuracy.

4. Enhancing Communication and Trust.

Effective communication is the foundation of expert-client interactions. Technology may increase this.

Transparency via Shared Access: Sharing files or dashboards promotes transparency and accountability.

Instant Updates: Push alerts from applications such as Slack or project management systems to keep customers up to date.

Multimedia communication: Videos, infographics, and interactive PDFs help people grasp complicated topics.

5. Creating immersive experiences

Digital technologies may turn boring discussions into fascinating experiences:

Virtual Reality (VR): Use VR platforms to build virtual worlds for hands-on learning or problem-solving.

Augmented Reality (AR) is the overlay of digital materials on real-world events, which is notably beneficial in domains such as design and teaching.

Gamification: Use gamified components, such as success badges or progress monitors, to inspire customers.

6. Automate Routine Tasks

Automation is a game changer, enabling specialists to concentrate on high-value tasks:

Email Campaigns: Use Mailchimp or ConvertKit to automate follow-ups, reminders, and newsletters.

Chatbots: AI-powered chatbots can answer simple questions, make appointments, and provide information.

Document Management: Use DocuSign or Adobe Sign to sign and share contracts and documents easily.

7. Using Analytics for Insightful Conversations

Data-driven insights may direct expert-client interactions and improve their effectiveness:

Behavioral analytics: Use technologies such as Hotjar to track how customers interact with content.

Performance Metrics: Use analytics dashboards to highlight client progress and pinpoint opportunities for improvement.

Predictive Analytics: Advanced AI systems may identify patterns and provide proactive answers.

8. Overcoming the Challenges of Technology Integration

Despite its benefits, technology integration may provide obstacles.

Technical Issues: Ensure that backup plans and technical help are readily accessible.

To avoid digital fatigue, alternate between digital engagements and personal touch points such as handwritten messages or phone conversations.

Learning Curve: Offer customers training and resources to help them adjust to new tools.

9. Creating a Secure Digital Environment.

Client confidence is based on the security of the platforms you utilize.

Data Encryption: Ensure that all conversations and data are encrypted.

Secure Authentication: Use two-factor authentication on sites that store sensitive information.

Comply with data protection standards such as GDPR or HIPAA, depending on your sector.

10. Continuous Improvement and Adaptation.

Technology is always growing, and keeping current is critical:

Stay Informed: Experiment with new tools and features to improve your offers regularly.

Solicit Feedback: Conduct surveys or have direct chats to determine what works and what doesn't.

Iterate: Continuously adjust your procedures in response to customer requests and technology developments.

11. Human Element in a Digital World

While technology is great, it's important not to lose the personal touch.

Empathy and Understanding: Use technology to strengthen, not replace, genuine human connections.

Face-to-face alternatives: To preserve a personal connection, meet in person sometimes or utilize video calls.

Celebrate Success: Use methods to recognize and celebrate achievements, instilling a feeling of accomplishment.

12. The Future of Expert-Client Interaction

The incorporation of developing technologies such as artificial intelligence, blockchain, and the metaverse promises to further transform expert-client discussions.

AI-Driven Personalisation: Experiences that are highly personalized to meet the requirements and preferences of each individual.

Blockchain for Transparency: Use blockchain technology to securely record agreements and follow progress.

Metaverse Meetings: Virtual places for immersive, collaborative talks that go beyond physical boundaries.

Integrating technology into expert-client engagements is more than simply using tools; it is about changing how we connect, collaborate, and generate value. When used correctly, technology improves communication, builds trust, and drives outcomes while keeping the essential human element at its heart. By embracing the digital revolution with purpose and strategy, experts can take their client connections to new heights, providing impact and innovation with each engagement.

The Future of Selling Expertise: Why Conversations Will Always Matter in a Digital Age

In a world increasingly dominated by algorithms, automation, and artificial intelligence, the importance of human connection remains ageless. While digital technologies and technical improvements have transformed how experts communicate with customers, the basis of selling expertise remains based on a single fundamental principle: honest, meaningful interactions. As we go forward, the art of communication will grow, becoming the differentiating element between success and mediocrity.

This conclusion delves into why discussions will always be necessary in selling knowledge, even in a digitally dominant world, and emphasizes the significance of always refining and modifying techniques to suit the demands of a changing marketplace.

Conversations Have the Power to Last

At the core of selling knowledge is a universal truth: people purchase from people they trust. No matter how sophisticated technology grows, trust is established through connection, comprehension, and conversation. Conversations continue to serve as a channel for trust, enabling experts to:

Understanding Client Needs: Conversations reveal complicated issues, emotions, and ambitions that no algorithm can truly grasp.

Establish authenticity: Genuine communication demonstrates competence, empathy, and trustworthiness in ways that cannot be mechanized.

Conversations foster long-term connections, changing one-time transactions into lasting collaborations.

The Digital Paradox: Technology Enhances Conversations

Rather than replacing human connection, technology enhances the effectiveness of discussions by:

Removing Barriers: Through virtual meetings and instant messaging, specialists may communicate with customers all around the world.

Improving Insights: Data-driven technologies give context, enabling more informed and targeted talks.

Increasing Efficiency: Automation handles regular activities, allowing you time for important conversations.

The difficulty resides in ensuring that these tools remain facilitators rather than replacements. The aim is to strike a balance between technological efficiency and true human connection.

Why Conversations Will Always Matter.

In this era of fast technological innovation, discussions are more important than ever. Here's why.

1. Emotional Connection.

Selling knowledge is more than just a transaction; it's extremely emotional. Clients need help not just to address issues, but also to be heard, supported, and understood. Conversations:

Validate the client's feelings and worries.

Provide comfort and clarity at times of uncertainty.

Create a rapport that goes beyond the digital environment.

2. The Power of Storytelling.

Stories—real-life examples, case studies, and compelling narratives—are the most effective ways to express expertise. Conversations set the setting for:

Sharing powerful success stories helps boost confidence.

Relating experiences to client issues.

Create a vision for the client's future success.

3. The Art Of Adaptation

Every customer is unique, and so are their requirements. Conversations enable experts to:

Adjust their strategy in real-time.

Delve further into unforeseen difficulties or possibilities.

Provide dynamic, customized solutions.

4. Trust in a Distrustful World.

Conversations are the cure to skepticism, which is fuelled by disinformation and impersonal algorithms. They humanize the process and create environments conducive to trust.

The Future of Sales Expertise

As we look forward, the landscape of selling expertise will continue to shift, led by three major trends:

1. Integrating Technology with Human Touch.

The future rests on achieving the ideal balance of technology and human interaction. Experts must

Use AI and automation to increase productivity while maintaining human participation for connection.

Use digital technologies to enhance talks rather than replace them.

Personalise interactions at scale to ensure that each customer feels appreciated.

2. Embracing continuous learning.

In a quickly changing world, being relevant requires agility. Experts must

Continuously improve their communication abilities to

meet changing client requirements.
Stay up to speed on technology advances to properly incorporate new tools.
Be proactive in learning about new customer demands and industry developments.

3. Concentrating on Value, Not Transactions

Clients are no longer looking for answers; they want significant, transformational experiences. Future conversations will focus on:

Providing long-term value above short-term remedies.

Leading clients on journeys of development, discovery, and empowerment.

Become valued partners rather than just service vendors.

Refine and adapt your approach.

The most effective specialists will be those who maintain agility and responsiveness.

Refining and adjusting your strategy involves:

Listening More Deeply: Prioritise active listening to genuinely comprehend the client's requirements and feelings.

Asking Better inquiries: Begin discussions with informative, open-ended inquiries that encourage discussion and discovery.

Being Present: Whether in person or online, give your full attention and real participation to every contact.

Embracing Feedback: Use customer feedback to always develop and expand your communication technique.

Investing in Soft Skills: Learn empathy, emotional intelligence, and narrative to improve the quality of your talks.

Conclusion: Timeless Skill in a Changing World.

The future of selling knowledge involves rethinking

rather than forsaking tradition. Conversations, the ageless cornerstone of human contact, will continue to form the basis of effective client relationships. Even as technology changes the world, the need for true, powerful interaction will continue.

By combining technology innovation with the art of communication, experts can build experiences that are not just efficient and scalable, but also genuinely personal and meaningful. The secret to prospering in the digital age is to embrace this duality: using technology while keeping the incomparable importance of personal connection.

Finally, the talks will create a lasting impact, motivate change, and foster the trust required to translate knowledge into long-term success. As the world changes, so must we—fine-tuning, adjusting, and never forgetting that the simple but profound act of speech is at the center of every effective relationship.

Summary: The Expertise Connection—Transforming Conversations into Client Commitment

In a world driven by technology and information overload, the value of true human connection is unparalleled. Conversations between experts and clients build trust, understanding, and commitment, transforming abstract information into actual value. These conversations go beyond commercial exchanges; they are transforming moments in which knowledge meets a client's innermost wants and goals.

The path from talk to commitment is seldom straightforward. It takes a combination of empathy, strategy, flexibility, and clarity. Your mission as a specialist is to become a trusted guide, illuminating the route to your client's objectives rather than just presenting answers. When conducted with clarity and purpose, these talks transcend the boundaries of business, becoming relationships based on mutual development and success.

Why Conversations Will Always Matter in the Digital Age.

The digital age has transformed communication by introducing solutions that improve speed and ease. However, the intricacies of face-to-face or voice-to-voice communication are what define meaningful relationships. Technology may enhance, but not replace, the trust-building power of a well-crafted discussion.

Clients are overloaded with information, alternatives, and automated systems. In the middle of this commotion, what they desire most is human connection—assurance that their specific issues are recognized and that their actions are backed by someone who actually cares. Your knowledge, conveyed via empathic and intelligent communication, is what cuts through the digital clutter.

Despite advances in artificial intelligence and machine learning, they cannot recreate the human traits that drive effective talks.

Emotional intelligence allows you to recognize and react to a client's unstated demands.

Authenticity promotes trust and rapport.

Ability to adapt to the unpredictable nature of human relationships.

The future of selling knowledge will be determined not by the most powerful algorithms, but by experts who can utilize technology to improve, not replace, their capacity to connect, communicate, and cooperate.

Continue to Refine and Adapt Your Approach.

Mastery of expert-client talks is a process, not a goal. Each connection provides a chance to learn, grow, and develop your approach. The most successful experts embrace adaptation and commit to lifelong learning.

Key Strategies for Ongoing Growth:

1. Seek Feedback: Following each interaction, consider what went well and where improvements may be made. Solicit honest feedback from customers to get new views.

2. Stay Curious: Continue to broaden your knowledge base, not just within your domain but

also in related fields. A wider range of skills allows for more in-depth discussions.

3. Use Technology Strategically: Use digital tools to improve preparation, follow-up, and client interaction. However, make sure that these tools are used in addition to, not instead of, actual discourse.

4. Practice Active Listening: Improve your capacity to listen intently, not just to words but also to tone, purpose, and underlying emotions. Active listening is one of the most effective methods for developing trust.

The Legacy of Expert-Driven Conversations.

At its core, the expertise relationship is about adding value—not just for the customer, but also for yourself as an expert. It is about establishing a legacy of trust, cooperation, and influence.

Each interaction you have has the potential to:
- Solve a problem.
- Create a relationship.
- Generate an idea.
- Change someone's life.

When your expertise becomes a transformational tool, your conversations turn into commitments, which then spread outward, forming a network of success stories.

Final Thoughts

Expertise is abundant in all industries, but connection is rare. The ability to turn conversations into commitments is what distinguishes exceptional professionals. It is a skill founded on comprehension, honed through practice, and elevated by authenticity.

As you move forward, remember that every client interaction is an opportunity to make a difference—not just by solving a problem, but also by becoming a trusted partner in their journey. You don't simply sell your expertise when you combine it with the art of communication; you also develop long-term connections, inspire confidence, and make a significant influence.

The world will continue to change, but the importance of true human connection will endure. Conversations matter. Commitment matters. And your skill, when presented with care, will always find its proper place.

Appendices: A Practical Toolkit for Mastering Conversations

The appendices provide a wealth of usable resources, including tools, motivation, and expertise to help you manage expert-client discussions. These parts are meant to enable you to put theory into practice, with worksheets to develop your approach, inspiring case studies, and tools to extend your knowledge.

Let's get into the main elements:

1. Worksheets for each conversation type.

These worksheets are designed to help you navigate and succeed in various sorts of expert-client discussions. These strategies help you develop trust, overcome obstacles, and close deals with structure and clarity.

Worksheet 1: Building rapport

Goal: Encourage trust and connection during early interactions.

Prompts:

What are the client's current problems or pain points?

How can I display comprehension and empathy?

What common interests or principles may I highlight?

Action Steps:

Determine the client's history and industry.

Prepare a tale or insight that relates to their aims.

Use active listening and mirroring strategies.

Reflection questions:

What instances of connection jumped out throughout this conversation?

How did I make the customer feel valuable?

Worksheet #2: Identifying Needs

Objective: Determine the client's underlying objectives and issues.

Prompts:

What open-ended inquiries can I ask to better understand their needs?

Are there any unstated issues I should address?

What solutions are aligned with their long-term goals?

Action Steps:

Deepen your understanding by asking "why" and "how" questions.

Make a customer needs map to identify pain areas and opportunities.

Reflection questions:

Did I truly comprehend the client's viewpoint?

What astonished me throughout our conversation?

Worksheet 3: Overcome Objections

Objective: Effectively manage resistance while preserving confidence.

Prompts:

What are the client's main complaints, and what is the underlying cause?

How can I reframe objections as opportunities?

Action Steps:

List possible concerns and develop evidence-based replies.

Role-play the discussion to improve your approach.

Reflection questions:

Did I respond to the criticism with empathy and logic?

How can I deal with similar concerns more effectively?

Worksheet 4: Close the Deal

Objective: Establish commitment while assuring mutual gain.

Prompts:

What are the client's main decision-making criteria?

Have I explained the value proposition clearly?

Action Steps:

Create a concise proposal showing the advantages and ROI.

Create a clear call to action and a follow-up strategy.

Reflection questions:

Have I made it simple for the customer to say "yes"?

How can I enhance my closing techniques?

Worksheet 5: Follow-up Conversations

Goal: Maintain the connection and encourage continuing interaction.

Prompts:

How can I deliver continuing value after the sale?

What input can I get to help enhance the relationship?

Action Steps:

Schedule frequent check-ins to ensure alignment.

Share useful thoughts, articles, or resources to help the customer.

Reflection questions:

What new demands or possibilities emerged?

How did the follow-up improve the relationship?

2. Case Studies on Successful Expert-Client Relationships

These real-world examples demonstrate the transformational impact of expert-client talks and illustrate fundamental ideas in action.

Case Study 1: Developing Trust with a Sceptical Client

Scenario: A financial counselor addressed a customer concerned about investing hazards.

Strategy:
Begin by actively listening to validate the client's worries.
Shared related success stories from customers with similar concerns.
To communicate difficult subjects, use simple, straightforward language.
The customer acquired confidence and trusted the adviser with their portfolio.

Case Study 2: Overcoming Objections in a Consulting Pitch.
Scenario: During a pitch to a tech firm, a consultant received criticism for their hefty prices.
Strategy:
Reframed the debate to emphasize ROI rather than expenses.
To alleviate immediate worries, we offered a flexible payment arrangement.
Provided a case study of a comparable startup that profited from their services.

Outcome: The company secured a contract, resulting in a 200% boost in operational efficiency.

Case Study 3: Turning a One-Time Engagement Into a Long-Term Partnership

Scenario: A career coach was originally engaged for a single session to develop a long-term connection.

Strategy:

Delivered outstanding value in the first session, delivering practical ideas.

Followed up with personalized resources and a plan for future development.

Maintaining regular contact demonstrates genuine interest in the client's success.

The customer enrolled in a year-long coaching program.

3. Suggested Readings and Resources

A carefully chosen mix of books, articles, and resources to help you understand and improve your abilities in expert-client engagements.

Books

"The Trusted Advisor" by David H. Maister, Charles H. Green, and Robert M. Galford
Insights on developing trusting relationships with customers.

Kerry Patterson et al.'s "Crucial Conversations: Tools for Talking When Stakes Are High"
Strategies for confidently conducting high-pressure talks.

Daniel H. Pink's "To Sell is Human: The Surprising Truth About Moving Others"
A new view on sales as a people-centered activity.

Articles

"The Psychology of Client Conversations" – Harvard Business Review
Examines the emotional and psychological aspects of client relationships.

"The Science of Listening: How to Unlock Client Needs" – Forbes

Tips for practicing active listening to discover hidden possibilities.

Digital Tools

CRM platforms, such as Salesforce or HubSpot, allow you to log customer interactions and personalize follow-ups.

Video conferencing: Use Zoom or Microsoft Teams to conduct flawless virtual meetings.

Mind Mapping Software: Tools such as MindMeister help clients see their requirements and solutions.

Final Thoughts: Empowering Your Journey.

The materials in this appendix are more than just tools; they are allies in mastering the art and science of expert-client communication. Using these exercises, examining real-life situations, and digging into suggested resources will provide you with the information and abilities you need to succeed in any conversation.

Remember that the pursuit of greatness is an ongoing process. With each discussion, you should adapt, grow, and perfect your approach. As you establish trust, overcome obstacles, and provide value, you will not only succeed but also create long-term, transformational connections that will define your legacy as an expert.

www.ingramcontent.com/pod-product-compliance
Lightning Source LLC
Chambersburg PA
CBHW050306230526
45471CB00005B/2041